TALKING ABOUT MYSELF

EATING DISORDERS

Interviews by Angela Neustatter
Photographs by Laurence Cendrowicz

FRANKLIN WATTS
LONDON • SYDNEY

First published in 2008 by Franklin Watts

Franklin Watts,
338 Euston Road,
London, NW1 3BH

Franklin Watts Australia,
Level 17/207 Kent Street,
Sydney, NSW 2000

Series editor: Sarah Peutrill
Art Director: Jonathan Hair
Design: Elaine Wilkinson
Additional research by: Charlotte Wormald
Panels written by: Sarah Ridley
Photographs: Laurence Cendrowicz (unless otherwise stated)

The Author and Publisher would like to thank the interviewees for their contributions
to this book.

Picture credits: Elke Dennis/Shutterstock: 13. Olly Hoeben: 16. Ingvald
Kaldhussater/Shutterstock: 20. nolie/Shutterstock: 11. Dimitrije Paunovic/Shutterstock:
9. Sveta San/Shutterstock: 23. Every attempt has been made to clear copyright. Should
there be any inadvertent omission please apply to the publisher for rectification.

Dewey number: 616.85'26
ISBN: 978 0 7496 7709 1

Printed in China

Franklin Watts is a division of Hachette Children's Books,
an Hachette Livre UK company.

CONTENTS

WHAT ARE EATING DISORDERS?

Food is essential to our bodies and enjoying a balanced, nutritious diet helps to give us energy and a zest for life. But for some people their relationship with food becomes distorted and the desire to eat very little or eat too much threatens their health and even their life.

Mental illnesses

Around 5% of girls in the UK have an eating disorder such as anorexia or bulimia. These are mental illnesses – they are caused by a disorder of the brain that results in a disruption in a person's thinking, feeling, moods and ability to relate to others. It is far less well known that boys and young men also get eating disorders. Although they only account for 10% of the total number of sufferers, the figure is rising.

Anorexia nervosa

Anorexia sufferers are convinced they are too fat, that their life would be better if they were slimmer. They may start with a normal calorie-controlled diet, but they then go further and intentionally starve themselves. The majority of anorexics deny that they have a problem, and some argue that they are just making a lifestyle choice.

Bulimia nervosa

Bulimia is another illness afflicting people who want to lose weight, but who choose to do it by binge-eating then vomiting or using laxatives to get rid of the food. Around half of all anorexics are bulimic as well.

How do these illnesses begin?

The feelings of despair and self-loathing which are often associated with these illnesses can be triggered by a range of things – although not every child or young person who experiences the triggers will react in this way. Anorexics are frequently perfectionists and never feel they can do well enough. So a lot of pressure or criticism can be a trigger. Bullying, particularly if it relates to body shape, rejection by friends, sexuality worries, family breakdown and abuse can all be triggers. It is also often said that anorexia and bulimia are ways people try to take control of their lives. The majority of males with eating disorders start cutting back as a result of being overweight and bullied.

What are the affects?

Bulimia and anorexia can both do a lot of damage to the body physically and emotionally. Eating disorders cause the highest number of deaths from mental health illness in the UK. They also damage the body's organs, destroy muscle, risk infertility and, in the case of bulimia, excessive vomiting can harm the lining of the throat. The longer the disorders go on, the harder

SIGNS OF BULIMIA AND ANOREXIA

Young adults with anorexia or bulimia can take a lot of care to hide their problem from their family and friends. Here are some signs to look out for:

• Weight loss or unusual weight changes

• Missing meals, eating very little, avoiding eating in public and large amounts of food disappearing in the home

• Exercising excessively

• Talking about being fat when they are normal or underweight

• Becoming preoccupied with preparing food and cooking for others

• Going to the toilet during or immediately after a meal

• Erratic moods: being withdrawn, quick to anger, very easily upset.

---

they are to treat. Sadly 40% of anorexics, even when they go for treatment and want to get better, never fully recover.

Obesity

The other side of eating disorders is overeating leading to obesity. Government figures show that one-third of children are overweight (weighing more than is normal or healthy) and that 15% of boys under 15 and just under 17% of girls are obese (extremely overweight, usually more than 30% over target weight). Compared to slim children, obese children are two times more likely to become overweight adults.

Obesity levels have risen steadily since the mid-1980s and this is thought, broadly, to be happening because pre-packaged, high-calorie meals are eaten far more than in the past. Furthermore children and young people take less exercise than in the past.

Being seriously overweight and obese puts pressure on the heart, leading to high blood pressure and diabetes. It is also a cause of much bullying and name-calling and the psychological effects can be devastating.

What can be done about eating disorders?

It can be difficult for a child or young person to deal with their problems and eating disorders alone. Ideally there will be help and support at home, but schools also have a large part to play in noticing when a child may be having issues around weight and food, and trying to help.

The government advises schools to encourage young people to eat at least five portions of fruit and vegetables a day, and to eat balanced levels of carbohydrates, proteins and dairy foods and not too much fat, sugar and salt. Regular exercise is also important.

This book

The young people interviewed in this book talk about their eating disorders and weight issues, explaining how they started, the effect on their lives and what has helped. Sadly, in many cases, these stories show how difficult it is to recover from an eating disorder once it has started. The stories also raise questions about the impact of the media on young girls in particular.

RECOVERING ANOREXIC

Leyla* began overeating as a child and was diagnosed with an eating disorder aged 12. She is now in recovery.

*Not her real name.

Q What was the attitude to food in your home?

My mother thought of herself as fat although she absolutely wasn't. But my father is overweight and eats a lot. He and my mother argued a lot about that. When I was about eight I began to hide crisps and biscuits in the bathroom and eat them before dinner. I started putting on weight and I minded.

Q Did you feel the need to be slim at school?

I had two very good friends and the ringleader of the three of us used to play us off against each other. It made me very insecure and I came to see other girls as thinner, prettier, happier and more popular.

"I came to see other girls as thinner, prettier, happier and more popular."

Q How was school?

I wasn't stupid but I dealt with my unhappiness by clowning around. My father went mad because I wasn't working hard enough although I was in the top ten.

Q What happened with your eating?

At Yom Kippur I fasted and realised it wasn't so hard so I cut out food a lot. I started walking great distances and taking laxatives in big doses. I cut out lunch at school but friends noticed and told my form teacher and that is how my parents found out.

Q When were you diagnosed with an eating disorder?

When I was 12. My parents took me to a psychiatrist. They tried hard to do nice things for me and my dad took me to the cinema and gave me sweets, which I ate. But when I got home I was in hysterics and my mother realised how ill I was. I went on losing weight and I went into an Eating Disorders Unit (EDU) during the Easter holidays when I was 13. I loved it. We had group therapy and art therapy. But it did me no good because I learnt a lot of tricks from people who had had eating disorders for 15 to 20 years.

"I learnt a lot of tricks from people who had had eating disorders for 15 to 20 years."

Q So that didn't cure you?

No. Next my parents tricked me into going to an in-patient EDU for three months. The philosophy was to feed you up. I learned to stick food on the roof of my mouth then go and spit it out, and other tricks so I lost weight. Then I was on supervision and never alone. Afterwards I went on holiday with my family in the summer and felt so fat I was determined to get thin again. I blamed them for letting me get that way. ▶

Q So what happened then?

I went back to school and being seen as thin and clever became an obsession. I worked very hard but when I went into year 12 I started making myself sick and that made me so unwell my dreams of getting As in Science and being an astronaut were ruined. My grades went down to Cs and Ds. I couldn't cope with this failure. That was when I started bringing up food and purging. I would not eat for five days of the week and I would drink diet fizzy drinks in the evenings. On Fridays I'd give Mum a huge list of foods I wanted and I'd binge all weekend, knowing I could bring it up.

I had a pair of jeans I'd bought in size double zero and they used to fall down. But I never saw I was thin. I got into Cambridge University and there my bulimia got out of control. I spent a fortune on food and sicked it up in the bathroom.

Q Did you have boyfriends?

I had a boyfriend in the second year. I got pregnant and had an abortion. But the boy wasn't concerned so that was that. My bulimia got yet worse. I used to leave sick around in bags. I had this room where I kept them and the ceiling was covered in flies.

"I had this room where I kept them and the ceiling was covered in flies."

Q So how have you moved on?

I suppose it was growing up. I moved into a place of my own which gave me a sense of personal responsibility and I began wanting to be healthy. I found a couple of understanding people to talk to and that helped. I rarely binge these days and I have learned to live with the weight I have gained. I never thought I could do it on my own, but I have. ■

ANOREXIA

Anorexia is an eating disorder that often starts with normal dieting but gets out of control. People with anorexia become obsessed with losing weight and being slim but cannot see how thin they have become. They often take an excessive amount of exercise, eat as little as possible and may use laxatives – all to continue losing weight. This weight loss may give them a feeling of control over their lives and/or make them feel more successful and attractive.

THE EFFECTS

However, depriving the body of food in this way stops it from functioning normally. People with anorexia may feel weak, constipated and depressed and they may grow fine body hair. Girls may lose their periods or have them irregularly. In the long term, the bones grow weak, the kidneys and heart can be damaged and there may be fertility problems.

RECOVERY

The first step to recovery is acknowledging there is a problem. Just talking to someone – whether it be a parent, friend, trained counsellor, doctor or psychologist – can help. For information on the treatment of eating disorders, see pages 21 and 25, as well as the websites of the organisations listed on page 31.

FIGHTING BULIMIA

Delia made herself bulimic aged 13. An unusual clinic for children helped her cope with eating.

I was a national swimmer and I became conscious of my body as a 12-year-old. The girls around all seemed to be skinnier than I was. My mum went on a diet and I thought I'd have a go too – it was something we could do together. I liked the routine of dieting. I lost weight slowly at first, then I started cutting out fat and other things. People were saying I looked really good as I got thinner so I didn't want to stop.

Becoming bulimic

I became bulimic when I was 13. I did it to stop my periods because they were interfering with my swimming. It was the only way I could eat in front of my parents and still lose weight. I hated doing it but I panicked as soon as I ate anything. It stopped my periods for several years.

I was rowing a lot with my parents but I felt a calm sense of control over food. If I had to have a meal I put food in my pockets, I hid it, I lied about it. I wore baggy clothes and if my parents weighed me I tied stones and weights around my body. I drank a lot of water to make me weigh more.

I knew I was too thin but I couldn't eat. I was living on lettuce and cucumber. I felt sure I would blow up. You aren't rational in this state.

Physically I couldn't do anything. I thought my legs would snap when I walked upstairs. I weighed just under 38 kg (six stone). I broke down and told my parents my real weight. When I got on the scales Dad went white. He took me to the GP and I was told I had three weeks to live.

"I was living on lettuce and cucumber. I felt sure I would blow up. You aren't rational in this state."

studying medicine was the best thing possible.
And I feel I can trust Mum with my problem now so
that's much better. But I haven't had a boyfriend yet.
I think it's very hard for me to let anyone touch me.
I suppose that's because I've spent so long disliking
my body and abusing it. ∎

"My first meal was a pizza. I got it down but afterwards I cried and cried."

Eating disorder clinic

I was referred to Rhodes Farm, which is an eating disorder clinic for children where there are nice activities like horse riding and swimming if you put on weight. I liked the look of that.

The philosophy was to get a lot of calories into you. My first meal was a pizza. I got it down but afterwards I cried and cried. I had breakfast and other meals – not having a choice made it easier. I was on 3,700 calories a day. I reached my target weight in 19 weeks.

But when I got home and my mother weighed my food and tried to make me eat macaroni cheese I had tantrums and kicked and screamed. Looking back I don't think my parents really understood and when Dad was having work problems I took it as an opportunity to starve again.

I went back to Rhodes Farm for my 17th birthday for three months. I wanted to go to university so I made an effort to eat. And since then when it gets difficult I have a weekend at Rhodes Farm to get me back on track. Getting to university where I'm

BULIMA

Bulimia is an eating disorder where someone craves food and 'binge-eats' – eating a lot of food quickly, and often secretly – and then vomits, or uses laxatives to get rid of the food. People with bulimia often have low self-esteem, difficult relationships with friends or family or have suffered a bereavement or other traumatic event. Eating a lot of food at once brings relief from these sad feelings but soon makes them feel miserable and guilty, which is why they then make themselves sick, or use laxatives. People with bulimia often also suffer from anorexia.

RECOGNISING BULIMIA

As their weight may not actually change much week-to-week, it may be difficult for parents or friends to notice that the person is bulimic. Spending a lot of time in the bathroom, especially straight after meals, is something to look out for.

EFFECTS OF BULIMIA

Bulimia can lead to tooth decay, irregular periods, sore throats, stomach aches, poor skin, tiredness and depression. Many people gradually cure themselves but others need to seek help from a doctor or a specialist – see page 31.

REACTION TO BULLYING

Tommy became worried about his weight at his all-boys school and stopped eating. He became seriously anorexic but has now regained a healthy weight.

Q **What led you to become anorexic?**

I went to an all-boys school and because I was overweight I got quite badly bullied about my body.

Q **How did this affect you?**

I began to feel physically worthless and to worry about my appearance. When I reached 16 and began to meet girls I felt very shy about myself. I assumed girls wouldn't like me.

"I began to feel physically worthless and to worry about my appearance."

Where did that thinking take you?

I became obsessed with the idea that if I could achieve the perfect body it would solve everything. I started dieting quite slowly. I just wouldn't eat chocolate and biscuits and things. Then I cut out bread and then meat. There were less and less things I would eat. I lost two stones (12.7kg) in two months and I went on down to about eight stones (50kg) which is pretty low as I am six foot one (1.85m) tall. I was also exercising a lot.

"I just wouldn't eat chocolate and biscuits and things. Then I cut out bread and then meat."

Did your parents notice?

My mum noticed fairly quickly that I was losing weight and she was very worried. She said she thought I had a problem. I knew she was right, inside, but I wouldn't admit it. I didn't know of boys having eating disorders. I stopped going out or seeing friends. It was as though I'd reverted to being a child. I read children's books. I think that was comforting because anorexia is complicated and you become very insecure and want things that make the world feel safer.

So how was your life at this point?

Everything had become a ritual. I would get up at 6.30a.m. and do 60 press-ups, 200 sit-ups and then repeat this before my shower. I would have a Weetabix and go to school. I would have an apple at lunchtime. In the evening I exercised more and I would eat some vegetables, but I didn't eat with my family.

How was your health?

I was pretty ill at this time. My body didn't have any muscle left because when your body doesn't have anything else to eat, it eats muscle. I had trouble getting upstairs and my heart was suffering.

How were your parents dealing with all this?

My father sort of ignored it. I think he found it difficult. My mother was very upset and in the end, because I couldn't bear seeing her so worried, I went to the doctor. I was referred on to a child mental health service in the NHS. I was told the strain I had put on my heart should have killed me. ▶

"I didn't know of boys having eating disorders."

> *"I can't tell you exactly why but one day I thought 'I don't want to do this any more'. I went home and ate everything I could find. It made me feel very ill but I couldn't stop."*

Q So were you hospitalised?

For a short time. But in fact by this time I was eating again. I can't tell you exactly why but one day I thought 'I don't want to do this any more'. I went home and ate everything I could find. It made me feel very ill but I couldn't stop. I put on 4kg (9 pounds) in a week. After that my weight see-sawed. I was probably about 57kg (nine stone) at this time. I wanted by now to get to a normal weight for my height. But even so it was a psychological battle for me to eat.

Q Did you overcome that battle?

If you've been anorexic I don't think you ever overcome it. But I made myself eat and drink body building drinks, and I reached a good weight and started going to the gym to build muscle. I went backwards once. I really wanted to go to drama school and I got a place. But I still had issues with food so sharing a room was tricky, and I wasn't that happy with the course. I started cutting back on food again and losing weight. So I left university and went home. I put on weight again. Now I'm about 70kg (11 stone) which is good.

> *"I wanted by now to get to a normal weight for my height. But even so it was a psychological battle for me to eat."*

BOYS AND EATING DISORDERS

Although there is less pressure on boys than girls to be slim, boys can develop eating disorders in their desire to change their body shape. Boys often mention being bullied or teased for being overweight, or trying to excel at certain sports, especially athletics, dance and horse-riding, as reasons why they developed a problem with eating. As with girls, difficult relationships with friends or family, pressure at school and low self-esteem can all trigger eating problems. All people with eating disorders tend to focus on food and losing weight, leaving little time to worry about other problems in their lives.

RECOGNISING A PROBLEM

Eating disorders amongst teenage boys and young adults are a growing problem but parents and doctors are less likely to suspect that anything is wrong. Boys are also more likely to hide the problem. Once an eating disorder has been recognised, help can come from many places by talking to parents, friends, a school nurse, a counsellor, a doctor or a dietician.

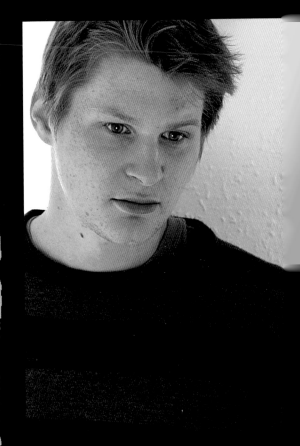

Q So what are the things you have learnt?

I think boys must talk about having an eating problem because at school when it should have been spotted, nobody said anything. If I'd been a girl I think people would have worried sooner. Growing up is scary and the prospect of having to work out what to do with your life can make you just want to find a way out. Starving yourself is that, but I can see now it's not the way to do it. ■

DANGEROUS IMAGES

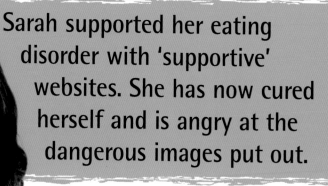

Sarah supported her eating disorder with 'supportive' websites. She has now cured herself and is angry at the dangerous images put out.

I stopped eating in my early teens because I was unhappy at school and at loggerheads with my parents. I felt very isolated so when I found the pro-ana and pro-mia websites where anorexics and bulimics discuss issues, share advice and reinforce each other I was happy to find others like me. Although some of what I saw shocked me. Fashion pictures of girls so thin you wondered how they were alive. And advice on how to go ever further with starvation.

"... after a few years I had vomited so much my throat lining disintegrated ..."

Bulimia

I started making myself sick. It seemed the only release when I was angry. But it was also dangerous: after a few years I had vomited so much my throat lining disintegrated and I went into anaphalactic shock if I ate anything I was allergic to.

I also became very depressed. My parents didn't know what to do. My mother tried very hard to get me to eat but I wouldn't. I just shut myself in my room and went on the websites. I was existing at one time on an apple and a Weetabix a day.

I had no friends at school and I really hated it. The worst was exam times when I got very stressed. My parents said it was fine to leave but I wanted to get my exams.

One day at a time

That was three years ago and I can't believe how much I have grown up. I think when I reached 18 I saw that I could never do what I wanted in life if I starved myself. So I said to myself, 'You are going to take one day at a time and make yourself eat, whether you like it or not.'

I started talking to my mum and my relationship with her and my dad improved. My mum didn't try to force me to eat and I stopped thinking she wanted to control my life.

I started having breakfast but I still wouldn't eat at school because I didn't like people seeing me eat. Sometimes I'd eat with my family in the evenings. Every day was different. I didn't notice feeling fitter until after three months I realised I wasn't crying every day and my mood had considerably improved.

But it's not quite so simple. I've done such harm to my organs than I will probably never be able to have children. I wanted to go to university but I didn't enjoy it at first as I was put into a flat with girls I didn't like at all. After a term and with exams coming up I felt I couldn't cope. Then I stopped eating again.

But I managed to break through that and most of the time now I can control my urge to starve. I still want to be thin but it doesn't bother me so much. In fact when I see images on 'YouTube' like the ones I looked at on the web it makes me really mad. ■

THE CULT OF THIN

Images of skinny models in fashion magazines, ultra-thin actresses and pop idols can make teenage girls very unhappy about their own bodies. It is easy to look at photographs or TV pictures and compare oneself unfavourably against them. Because more attention is often given to how media stars look than to what they say or do, it can seem as if appearance is all that matters.

NATURAL GOOD LOOKS?
While many models are naturally very slim and tall, they also spend a lot of time exercising and pampering their bodies. Before a photoshoot, hairdressers and make-up artists work wonders on skin and hair, while photographers use lights and certain angles to make people look even taller or slimmer. Graphic designers also work to improve photographs. A great deal of work goes into the apparently effortless good looks that appear in magazines or on screen.

Unfortunately, the pressure to be ultra-slim has caused some actresses, pop stars and fashion models to develop eating disorders. Sadly, a few have even died. There are now moves within the fashion industry to ban seriously thin models from the catwalk – both for their own health, and for those who are affected by the message they put out.

SYMPTOM OF DEPRESSION

Helen sees now that having a brother with special needs and an unwell mother may have contributed to her eating disorder. She has been in and out of eating disorder units.

Q How was your childhood?

I think it was happy although with stresses. My brother, two years older, was profoundly disabled and I found it hard to get close to my parents because there were so many practical issues taking their time, coping with my brother. Also my mother has a degenerative lung disease. But it was only later on when I saw a counsellor that the idea all this might have had an impact on my behaviour came up.

Q So when did you stop eating?

I was feeling kind of depressed when I was 13 and I couldn't see why. But I saw my dad lose weight on a

"I was feeling kind of depressed when I was 13 and I couldn't see why."

diet and he seemed more contented, so I decided I was fat and life would be better if I lost weight. I tried Dad's way of having just a piece of fruit for lunch, then I started cutting more foods out. Once I had made the decision to stop eating it was quite straightforward. I did get hungry but I ignored it. I felt I was doing something about my unhappiness.

Q Did you lose weight quickly?

I didn't weigh myself and it came as a surprise when my mother said I was looking very thin. And a teacher at school spoke to me about it. When I was weighed I had gone from seven and a half stone (48kg) to five stone ten (36kg). The teacher phoned my mum who took me to a doctor. I was beginning to realise things were out of control because I was fooling people I was eating. I felt very tired and my periods had stopped.

"... things were out of control because I was fooling people I was eating."

Q So what happened?

I was referred to a dietician and I saw the school counsellor. That was helpful. It was the first time I had spoken about it to anyone and they seemed so caring. I started eating more regularly and my weight stabilised but I didn't gain weight. So after a few months I was referred to an eating disorders clinic where they told me and Mum I could drop dead at any moment. That really upset her but I didn't believe it. The good thing was Mum started talking to me more after that. ▶

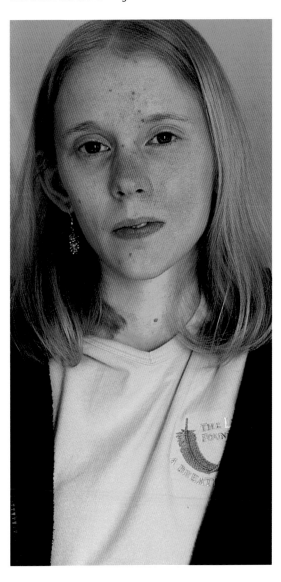

Did things improve at this point?

No. I didn't gain weight and I was referred to an in-patient unit but I made a deal with them that I could stay at home and go to school if I put on weight. I started using body-building drinks and I did manage to put on some weight but I remained below my target weight. I felt I was at war with people trying to force me to be someone I didn't want to be.

I was lying about eating to my dietician, and this went on for about a year by which time I think everyone was fed up with me. I was fed up with the situation too and I was becoming more depressed again. So when my GCSEs were over I went to an in-patient unit thinking I'd get my weight to a healthy level and be done with it. I neglected to tell them I was depressed so they just focused on feeding me while I was learning tricks from the other, more experienced, anorexics to avoid gaining weight. I left without being discharged and lost weight.

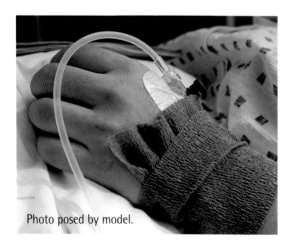

Photo posed by model.

Did they leave you to it then?

Not at all. I was sectioned the week before Christmas aged 16. My depression was very bad and they put me on Prozac, which I have been on ever since, although I did overdose on it when my brother died. I just felt in despair and the world seemed to be collapsing. But that was very bad – I had panic attacks, I shook for days, couldn't think and felt dreadful. I ended up on the unit and I did gain weight. I took my A' levels. I insisted on going to university even though I was advised against it. It was harder being away from home than I had expected. I felt very isolated and didn't want to socialise.

What happened to your weight at university?

I stopped eating and the university refused to keep me. But having low weight was more important to me. I went to work doing administration in the place my mother worked. I liked that, but my psychologist was worried I wasn't gaining the necessary weight and sent me back to the unit. I was so upset I tried to hang myself from the banisters. I was sectioned again, tube fed in hospital and then I returned to the eating disorders unit and discharged once my weight was satisfactory.

So did you keep it that way at home?

It's stayed that way so far and I'm managing better than I expected. Most of the time I accept this is how

"I was sectioned again, tube fed in hospital and then I returned to the eating disorders unit."

> "I sometimes look back
> on all this and wish
> I hadn't started,
> although I can't imagine
> a different life."

it has to be although the idea of dying is not so bad. But I am close to my mum now and don't want to cause her any more pain. I sometimes look back on all this and wish I hadn't started, although I can't imagine a different life. But I do belong to BEAT – the eating disorders organisation and I volunteer to speak about my experience. If there's a single thing I'd say it's that an eating disorder isn't a great life choice. ■

TREATING EATING DISORDERS

If someone is suffering from a persistent eating disorder that they cannot get over on their own, or with the help of family or friends, they need to see their doctor. A doctor (GP) will talk to the person and assess their weight and general health. Depending on the findings, the doctor might arrange meetings with a counsellor or psychologist, suggest a course of antidepressants, and/or arrange for advice from a dietician. The doctor will continue to monitor the general health of the person while he or she receives help from other people. In some cases, it might be necessary to seek in-patient care (see page 25).

ACCEPTING HELP

Counsellors and psychologists are trained to listen and give advice. They will talk to the person about their relationship with food and about other areas of life that might be causing difficulties. A dietician is an expert on nutrition and can give good advice on eating habits and on how to regain and maintain an acceptable body weight.

FROM OBESE TO BULIMIC

Sarah was an overweight child and became bulimic to deal with it. She found release in drama but still struggles with her illness.

Q When did weight become a problem?

As a child I was overweight and at puberty I became badly asthmatic and I was put on steroids. I put on a lot of weight and became clinically obese.

Q How did that affect you?

People stared. Adults and children made abusive comments and I spent a lot of time trying to avoid being seen. I don't think my parents realised how I was feeling.

"People stared. Adults and children made abusive comments and I spent a lot of time trying to avoid being seen."

> "I was doing A' levels and on a pattern of starving by day, bingeing in the evenings and taking laxatives."

So what happened then?

was 14 when the idea of making myself sick after ting came into my head. I felt tremendous relief. lso restricted my food and got up at 6am to exercise. s I lost weight I learnt how much praise it brings. ople told me how good I looked and a teacher said I ust feel really good because I'd got thinner. I was termined to lose more weight. I was doing A' levels d on a pattern of starving by day, bingeing in the enings and taking laxatives.

> 'd developed a sugar addiction nd I was living on adrenaline. I felt completely exhausted, weak, I had palpitations and was breathless."

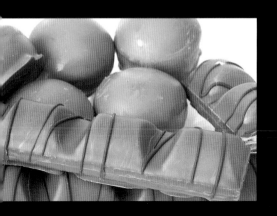

Did you think of getting help?

I had joined the local youth theatre, because acting was the one thing that made me feel good. I could be somebody else and I was good at it. The National Youth Theatre accepted me and that was a massive boost to my confidence. I didn't throw up for a week. Then to cap it all I won a bursary and an award for my work and finally I got into the Guildhall School of Music and Drama which was the thing I most wanted. But I was still on my crazy starvation cycle. I remember writing in my diary about what would happen if I didn't sort myself out.

Did you sort yourself out?

I didn't. In fact I lived in a flat with a guy who was 139kg (22 stone) and dieting frantically. We were weight-loss buddies and that was disastrous. I began to feel weak and very low. This was not helped by the fact I was taking speed to get through the long college days. My tutor spotted something wrong and she took me to the college counsellor. But that didn't work. I just sat there in a room for an hour with a man who looked at his feet and said nothing. I was referred to an out-patients eating disorders unit. I was given some cognitive behavioural therapy, which helped me stop blaming myself for what I was doing. But in my third year at Guildhall things went wrong. I'd developed a sugar addiction and I was living on adrenaline. I felt completely exhausted, weak, I had palpitations and ▶

was breathless. I hated myself and wished I could die
had all the things I'd so wanted and I had turned
myself into a wreck.

Q How did you cope with acting?

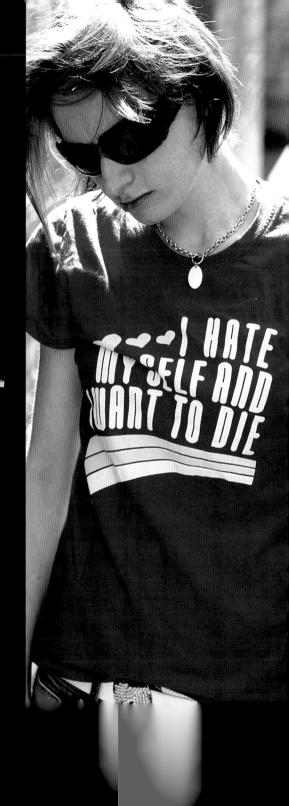

didn't. I went home to live with my parents and I
lost yet more weight. I had a big row with my dad so
he got me a flat but I just spent the days eating and
throwing up. I was admitted to a psychiatric unit and
t was here that the biggest stroke of luck happened.
They told me about Clean Break, an organisation that
runs drama courses and puts on projects to help
women in difficulties use their creativity to move
forward. I got on to one of the courses they run.
t was very engaging and the place was nurturing.
They gave us lunch money and that felt okay so I
ate and kept the food down.

> "I went home to live with
> my parents and I
> lost yet more weight."

Q So was that the end of your eating disorder?

wish it was so easy. I was still binging at the end
of the day. But I did get a lot of confidence back
and my acting skills returned. I joined an Overeaters
Anon group because I still had my eating problems
and I was employed as an acting mentor by Cardboard
Citizens, a performing company made up from
homeless people. I was still eating and vomiting a bit,
but having a job and being paid helped quite a bit.

> "I just wish I had never started being so determined to lose weight."

Even so you are struggling again?

Yes, I just couldn't seem to eat and keep it down. I collapsed and ended up in A and E. From there I was sent to a psychiatric unit when what I really needed was a dedicated eating disorders unit and to stay long enough that I had to get better. I just wish I had never started being so determined to lose weight. I had no idea it would destroy my life in the way it has so far. ■

IN-PATIENT CARE

Sometimes it is necessary for someone with an eating disorder to accept in-patient care. Their body weight might have reached a dangerously low level, or they may have become so low in themselves that they are thinking of suicide.

CLINICS

There are various clinics around the country that focus on eating disorders and will help the person to return to health. They vary in their exact timetables but most focus on regulating eating habits to prevent any further weight loss and bring the person back to a better body weight. There may be classes about nutrition and diet.

THERAPY

As an in-patient, there will be many opportunities to talk about feelings, both in relation to food and to life in general. There will be group therapy, where several young people help each other by talking about their lives with the help of a therapist. There may be family therapy sessions, when the family will visit and talk about family relationships in an attempt to improve life at home. Individual appointments with a psychologist or counsellor will help to look at the particular situation of each person. In addition, there will be activities to remove the focus from food, as well as schooling for those who are still in full-time education.

FIGHTING OBESITY

Jordan,13, put on weight as he grew towards puberty and was becoming self-conscious about it. He joined the MEND (Mind, Exercise, Nutrition) programme designed to fight obesity in children and through this has lost weight.

I was beginning to dislike how big I had become. It made me self-conscious so I held back from joining in sports and physical activities with my friends at school. My mum began to get worried because she had seen my sister put on weight and get quite large and she had not liked being that way. Mum didn't want the same to happen to me.

> "It made me self-conscious so I held back from joining in sports and physical activities with my friends ..."

First session

My aunt saw an article about the MEND programme which has become one of the most successful anti-obesity programmes for young people, apparently. My mum wasn't sure about how I'd feel doing two sessions a week for nine weeks – and a parent has to be involved too. She told me that was quite a commitment for her after a day's work.

I didn't feel too bad when I went to the induction session because there were about 12 children, some a lot larger than me. We all introduced ourselves and then we did some outdoor activities. The first session of the week was always a discussion about food: what we eat, what the food is and what it does to you;

why some foods make you fat; healthy and nutritional eating. Parents were encouraged to cook meals, rather than buying fast-food and to cook lots of vegetables. My mum started making recipes they give you and I liked those. In the second session we always did physical activities – games, sports, swimming. I didn't find it too hard. I stopped drinking fizzy drinks and had water instead, and I didn't buy crisps or chocolate.

Slow start

I didn't lose weight easily. At first it was very slow and I felt a bit despondent, but then I realised it was coming off and by the end I had lost 15cm off my waist. I was aware of feeling better and having more energy and as I got good at sports I could see how my weight had stopped me trying before.

Parental support

It was good having my mum involved, she told me later how hard it had been before seeing kids teasing me and that I was becoming self-conscious about being big. My dad was very supportive too. One day my mum saw me coming out of a shop carrying crisps and she pounced on me ready to be cross, but then she saw they were low-fat crisps and she just laughed.

I have finished with MEND but I've learnt to think about what I eat – Mum says I used to eat anything and everything! I limit myself to a single portion at dinner. I've kept up the swimming and I take a cousin who is younger and quite big because I know it would make him feel better if he slimmed down. I guess in a way it's become a mission to help other kids if they have a weight problem. ■

OBESITY

Obesity is the medical term used to describe someone who is seriously overweight. Being obese can lead to many health problems, including heart disease, cancer, osteoarthritis, diabetes and depression. It is one of the biggest health problems in the UK and the number of obese children has tripled in the last 20 years – 17% of 15-year-olds are now clinically obese.

DIAGNOSING OBESITY

The body mass index is used to work out whether someone is clinically obese by measuring their weight against their height and sex. To find out your own body mass index (BMI), visit your doctor or go to one of the many websites (including the MEND website listed on page 31) where the information can be typed into the computer to give a result.

LOSING WEIGHT

If you have a weight problem, ask your doctor for help in the first instance. It is important to lose weight slowly and sensibly – without trying extreme or fad diets. The basic rule is to look at lifestyle and diet – and change both. Increase the amount of exercise you take and decrease the amount of food you eat, especially fatty and sugary foods. There are many websites that give advice on how to lose weight.

FEELING GOOD AT LAST

Barbara* went through several years being overweight and very self-conscious. Finding her direction in life means she is happy with her body.

*Not her real name.

"I began to feel self-conscious about the clothes I could wear."

I was an average-sized child and my parents always stressed the importance of being healthy but also happy. But I was at an all-girls secondary school and the lunches were very unhealthy. I'd learnt not to be a fussy eater so I ate what there was. Age 11 I began putting on weight and until I was 13 I thought I was just growing and several of us were becoming pudgier. But I was aware that every time I weighed myself, which wasn't often, I seemed to be a stone heavier than I remembered the time before. Then I began to feel self-conscious about the clothes I could wear. No more minis for example. I stopped feeling excited about dressing up to go out. I looked for clothes that would hide my body.

Getting bigger

I was aware of anorexia, it was very prevalent around me and I could see how destructive it was. But I just kept putting on weight. I didn't like going to swimming pools with friends and that kind of thing because I felt self-conscious. I compensated by being very gregarious and acting as though it didn't bother me, but underneath it did. I wanted to lose weight but didn't have the willpower.

"My weight really wasn't the problem — after all I had friends when I was fat and when I was slim."

I went to university and had hoped to get slimmer first but I didn't manage and my weight seemed to come into everything. If I went out to lunch I was aware of people seeing me as big, and I was self-conscious in case they were watching me eat. I didn't have a boyfriend but my mum helped with her attitude that it just wasn't my time.

But then when I was 20 and having time off univeristy I met a man seven years older. Then I felt very self-conscious about being overweight, but this man transformed that feeling by telling me I was very attractive and lovely. And because I felt good with him I ate less – I suppose I didn't need food as comfort at that time. My weight began to go steadily down. I was aware of enjoying going clothes shopping and to the pub with friends. But I was then given a hard time by people who said I had lost too much weight. It was confusing. At the same time the relationship was proving problematic and I began to realise that having got into university to do medicine – something that pleased my parents who are both medical – it wasn't what I really wanted. I left university but felt a failure.

Feeling good

A friend urged me to do an A' level in English Literature as that was the thing I had always loved. I did this and got a good mark. I immediately felt better with my life even though my relationship broke up. I put on weight again but this time I was feeling good about myself and it didn't feel problematic.

What I learnt from all this was that my weight really wasn't the problem – after all I had friends when I was fat and when I was slim. Nobody rejected me. The important thing was finding my direction and feeling good about what I was doing with my life. I am happy with my body for the first time in years. ■

GLOSSARY

A and E
The department in a hospital where accidents and emergencies are treated.

adrenaline
A natural stimulant that causes increases in the heart's rate and how hard it contracts.

cognitive behavioural therapy
A talking treatment that emphasises the important role of thinking in how we feel and what we do. The treatment involves identifying how negative thoughts affect us and then looks at ways of tackling or challenging those thoughts.

laxatives
Medications that are prescribed to relieve long-term constipation (infrequent or abnormally delayed movement of the bowels), but which are sometimes abused in order to lose weight.

NHS (National Health Service)
The system of free medical services for residents of the UK. The NHS is financed through taxes.

Nutrition
The taking in and use of food and other nourishing material by the body. The nutrients contained in this food are extracted, absorbed and then used as "fuel" for growth, repair, movement, thinking, and for many other bodily functions.

obese
A condition in which your weight is much more than it should be for your height, and in which the percentage of body fat is also considerably in excess.

palpitations
A sensation of pounding or fluttering in the chest.

Prozac
An antidepressant drug that is used in the treatment of depression, body dysmorphic disorder, obsessive-compulsive disorder, bulimia nervosa and other disorders.

psychiatrist
A medical doctor who specialises in the diagnosis and treatment of mental disorders.

sectioned
A person is sectioned when they are detained, against their will, under the Mental Health Act, for hospital treatment.

self-esteem
Self-esteem is how we think and feel about ourselves. This includes how we think about the way we look, our abilities and our relationships with others. We are not born with self-esteem it is something we develop.

speed
An illegal drug. It usually somes as a grey, white or dirty white powder. It may also come in tablet form. It can be snorted, swallowed, injected or smoked.

steroids
Steroids are a particular type of chemical. Many are found naturally in the body, but synthetic steroids are manufactured for treating diseases, including asthma. Some steroids are sometimes used by athletes to build up their muscles and in some cases may be mis-used.

sugar addiction
A popular term for the situation where individuals crave sweet foods, and find them impossible to give up.

Yom Kippur
The Jewish day of atonement – a very solemn day devoted to fasting, prayer, and repentance.

FURTHER INFORMATION

ORGANISATIONS & HELPLINES

Beat
Helpline: 08456 341414
Web: www.b-eat.co.uk
The UK's leading eating disorder charity. The organisation campaigns, challenges the stigma people with eating disorders face, and gives people the help and support they need.

Capio Helpline
Free helpline: 0800 733 094
Web: www.florencenightingale
hospitals.co.uk
Advice on anorexia or bulimia, addictions, depression etc.

Careline
Tel: 0845 122 8622
Web: www.carelineuk.org
Telephone counselling for people of any age, on any issue.

ChildLine
Free helpline: 0800 1111
Web: www.childline.org.uk
Telephone counselling for any child with any problem.

Eating disorders centre
Tel: 0845 838 2040
Web: www.eating-disorders.org.uk
The National Centre For Eating Disorders offers counselling, self help, professional training and support.

Get Connected
Free helpline: 0808 808 4994
Web: www.getconnected.org.uk
Helpline for young people.

MEND Programme
Tel: 0870 609 1405
Web: www.mendprogramme.org
One of the UK's most innovative and effective obesity prevention and treatment programmes.

Rethink
Helpline: 020 8974 6814
Web: www.rethink.org
Services to carers and people with severe mental illness.

Rhodes Farm
Tel: 020 8906 0885
Web: www.rhodesfarm.com
The treatment centre that Delia attended (see pages 10-11).

Samaritans
Tel: 08457 90 90 90
Web: www.samaritans.org.uk
Support for anyone in crisis.

SANE
Tel: 08457 678000
Web: www.sane.org.uk
For sufferers, friends and relatives affected by mental illness.

There4me
Web: www.there4me.com
Email support service for young people between 12-16 years.

Threshold Women's Mental Health Infoline
Web: www.thresholdwomen.org.uk
Information for those concerned about women's mental health (16+).

Youth Access
Helpline: 020 8896 3675
Web: www.youthaccess.org.uk
Counselling services for young people aged 12–25 years.

Youth2Youth
Web: www.youth2youth.co.uk
Email and telephone support, run by young volunteers for under 19s.

FURTHER WEBSITES

www.bbc.co.uk/health/healthy_living/nutrition/
Useful information on healthy eating.

www.rcpsych.ac.uk/mentalhealth
information.aspx
Click on the links to access useful leaflets on anorexia and bulimia.

www.youngminds.org.uk
The young people's mental health charity.

www.thesite.org
Articles on young people's issues including health and wellbeing.

AUSTRALIA/NEW ZEALAND

www.kidshelp.com.au
Free helpline: 1800 55 1800
Telephone and online counselling for young people under 25.

www.youthline.co.nz
Support for young people in New Zealand.

INDEX

TALKING POINTS

The interviews in this book may provoke a range of reactions: shock, sympathy, empathy, sadness. As many of the interviewees found, talking can help you to sort out your emotions. If you wish to talk about the interviews, here are some questions to get you started.

Leyla's story - page 6
How do you think Leyla's parents' relationship with food affected her? How much pressure do you think teenage girls face to be thin?

Delia's story - page 10
Why do you think Delia dislikes her body? What do you think of the philosophy of Rhodes Farm? Would it work for anyone?

Tommy's story - page 12
Why do you think bullying is often the cause of boys developing an eating disorder? Is it more likely that others would have recognised his problem if he was a girl?

Sarah's story - page 16
Sarah thinks images in the media contribute towards eating disorders. How far do you agree or disagree with this?

Helen's story - page 18
Helen didn't realise that her family situation had an impact on her. Why do you think this is?

Sarah's story - page 22
Sarah has very low self-esteem stemming from childhood. What things might help her improve this?

Jordan's story - page 24
Many people try - and fail at - dieting. What do you think helped Jordan to suceed? Why do you think obesity is such a relatively recent problem in western countries?

Barbara's story - page 28
Barbara was always very self-concious about her weight but now has a more balanced perspective. What helped her do this? Would you say she had an eating disorder in the same way as the other people in this book?

These are the lists of contents for each title in *Talking About Myself:*

Depression
What is depression? • All alone • Love's lost • Drug-taking depression • Accepting the past • Years of depression • Managing meltdown - bipolar disorder • Pushy parent • Attempted suicide

Eating Disorders
What are eating disorders? • Recovering anorexic • Fighting bulimia • Reaction to bullying - male anorexia • Dangerous images • Symptom of depression • From obese to bulimic • Fighting obesity • Feeling good at last

Losing a loved one
Coping with loss • Living with guilt • Losing a brother • Keeping a friend in mind • Caring for my mother • Holding on to memories - losing a granddad • Coping with a tragic death • Hearing from abroad • Feeling betrayed

My family
What is a family? • Dealing with divorce • When my parents split up • Father and son difficulties • Keeping the peace • Difficult at any age • Meeting my father for the first time • Care and adoption • Caring for my mother

Racism
What is racism? • Trying to belong - a Muslim's story • Culture clash • Being the outsider • Anti-Semitic attack • Bullied by other Muslims • Breaking down racism • Not allowed to mix • Growing up with racism

Relationships & Sex
First relationhips • Sleeping around • Sex without attachment • Glad to be gay • Dealing with homophobia • Losing my relationships confidence • Becoming a single parent • Young father • Childhood abuse

WIDE WORLD

PEOPLE *of the*
RAIN FORESTS

Anna Lewington and Edward Parker

WAYLAND

WIDE WORLD

PEOPLE *of the* **GRASSLANDS**
PEOPLE *of the* **DESERTS**
PEOPLE *of the* **ISLANDS**

PEOPLE *of the* **MOUNTAINS**
PEOPLE *of the* **POLAR REGIONS**
PEOPLE *of the* **RAIN FORESTS**

Cover: A Belaga-Kenyab woman from Sarawak, Borneo, collecting medicinal rainforest plants.

Title page: Children in the Philippines at the window of their reed hut, built with palms and other rainforest materials.

This page and Contents page: An area of tropical rain forest in the Amazon region, South America.

Book editor: Liz Harman
Series editor: Polly Goodman
Designer: Mark Whitchurch
Consultant: Anne Marley, Principal Librarian, Children and Schools Library Service, Hampshire

First published in 1997 by
Wayland Publishers Ltd
61 Western Road, Hove
East Sussex, BN3 1JD, England

Find Wayland on the Internet at
http://www.wayland.co.uk

British Library Cataloguing in Publication Data
Parker, Edward
    People of the Rain Forests. – (Wide world)
    1. Rain forests – Juvenile literature
    2. Rainforest ecology – Juvenile literature
    3. Human ecology – Juvenile literature
    I. Title II. Harman, Liz
    577.3'4

ISBN 0 7502 2019 8

Typeset by Mark Whitchurch
Printed and bound in Eurografica

Contents

Introduction

The world's rain forests are often thought of as wild, mysterious places full of giant plants and dangerous animals. However, people have lived in rain forests for hundreds of thousands of years and today they are home to a population of about 140 million. Rainforest people live in settlements ranging from traditional rainforest villages to huge cities.

Rainforest Facts

Biggest rain forest:
 Amazon, South America
Wettest rain forests:
 Hawaii and Cameroon: over 6 m rain a year
Area covered by tropical rain forest:
 8.5 million km²
Area covered by temperate rain forest:
 15–20 million hectares

Rainforest people

Rainforest people come from a variety of racial backgrounds and have many different lifestyles. Some are called indigenous or tribal people. They are the descendants of the very first people who lived in rain forests thousands of years ago. Many indigenous people have a very traditional lifestyle, hunting and growing the food that they need. Some rainforest dwellers are migrants, who have moved to the rain forest in search of land where they can grow enough food to feed their families. Others move to rain forests looking for jobs in industries like mining, logging and cattle ranching.

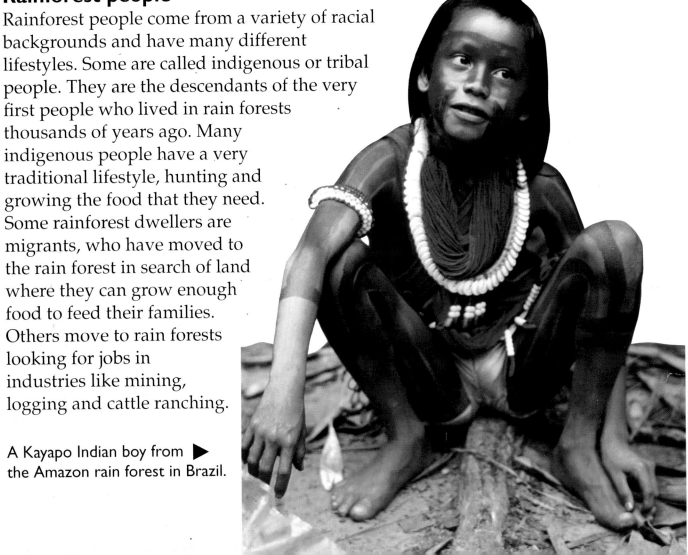

A Kayapo Indian boy from ▶ the Amazon rain forest in Brazil.

Rainforest destruction

Rainforest populations are increasing, but the rain forests themselves are being destroyed, as they are cut down for logging or to make room for crops, roads, settlements and cattle ranches. Both indigenous and more recent rainforest peoples are living in a changing environment and the future is uncertain.

A worker on an oil well in the forest of Gabon, ▶ West Africa. Oil is one of many resources in the rain forests which provides work for people.

▼ Caracas, the capital of Venezuela in South America, is a huge city surrounded by rain forest.

What is a Rain Forest?

Rain forests are forests that grow in constantly wet conditions. Generally, forests that have more than 2,000 mm of rain (moisture) evenly spread throughout the year are considered to be rain forests.

Rain forests can be divided into two main types: tropical and temperate. But there are many different types of tropical and temperate rain forest. Even experts find it difficult to say where one rainforest type stops and another begins.

Tropical rain forests

Tropical rain forests are hot and wet. They can be found around the Equator, between the Tropics of Cancer and Capricorn. About 90 per cent of the world's tropical rain forests are found in the Amazon region of South America, and in Central Africa and Southeast Asia.

▼ This map shows the main areas where the world's rain forests are located.

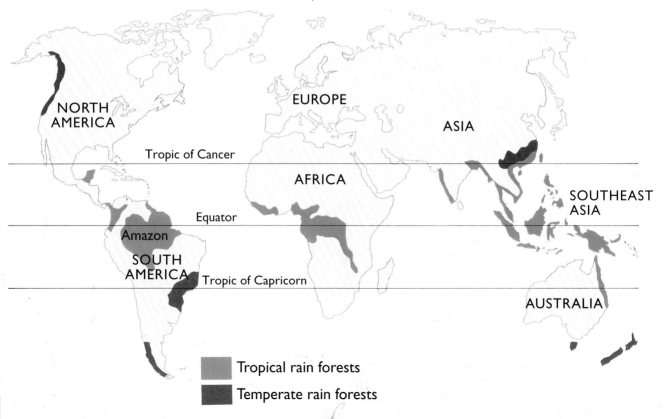

NORTH AMERICA

EUROPE

ASIA

Tropic of Cancer

AFRICA

SOUTHEAST ASIA

Equator

Amazon

SOUTH AMERICA

Tropic of Capricorn

AUSTRALIA

Tropical rain forests

Temperate rain forests

In the flooded forest in the ▶ upper Amazon of Brazil, people organize their lives to fit the seasons.

Tropical rain forests are often divided into two main types: hot, humid lowland forests and cooler, damper montane forests, which are found above 900 m. Examples of lowland forest include flooded forest and mangrove forest.

Mangroves line one quarter of the world's tropical coastlines. There are fifty-five different types of mangrove forest, covering an area of approximately 2,400 km². Mangrove forests give coastlines vital protection from waves, as well as providing a sheltered environment where thousands of water creatures breed.

▼ The Amazon rain forest is the world's largest single area of rain forest, covering large expanses in countries like Venezuela.

Tropical Treasure Houses

Tropical rain forests are famous for their amazing variety of plant and animal life. Although they only cover 6 per cent of the earth's surface, tropical rain forests are home to more than half of the world's animal and plant species. In a typical 10 km² patch of forest, scientists expect to find 1,500 species of flowering plants, 750 kinds of trees, 400 bird species and more than 150 types of butterflies.

Temperate rain forests

Temperate rain forests lie north and south of the tropics, where the rainfall is just as high but the temperature is cooler. Temperate rain forests can be found in southern Chile and along the north-west coast of North America, almost as far north as the Arctic Circle. Small but important areas of temperate rain forest can also be found in Tasmania, New Zealand and even in China.

Climate and lifestyle

Rain forests are very wet and some have heavy rain almost every day. Because of this heavy rainfall, rainforest people often build their houses on stilts to keep them above the wet ground. In one part of the Amazon rain forest, the water level of the rivers and lakes can rise by 13 m in the wet season. The heavy rain can even wash away roads.

In tropical rainforest cities where there are fewer trees to provide shade and absorb heat, many offices and homes have air conditioning systems which keep the buildings cool in the fierce heat of the Sun.

The importance of rain forests

Rain forests are vitally important to every human being on earth. They provide timber, food, medicine and many raw materials that are vital to industries around the world. Rain forests also allow all life on earth to thrive by helping to maintain the balance of the gases in the atmosphere, which helps to control the climate.

▼ Rainforest dwellers have used plants as medicines for centuries. This Belaga-Kenyab woman, in Sarawak, Borneo, is collecting a plant used to treat fevers.

Disappearing Forests
More than half of the world's rain forest has disappeared in the last fifty years. Tropical rain forests are being destroyed at a rate of about 142,000 km² per year. Temperate rain forests now cover less than half of their original area of 300,000–400,000 km². It is estimated that, in about twenty years' time, the only large expanses of rain forest left will be found in the Congo and Amazon river basins.

▲ Typical tropical rainforest vegetation in Costa Rica.

The red-eyed tree frog is one ▶ of thousands of animal species found in the world's rain forests.

▲ An Asmat man in Irian Jaya, Indonesia, fishing in a mangrove forest. Mangrove forests are rich in fish, which provide food for forest dwellers.

The 140 million people who live in, or close to, the world's rain forests benefit directly from their environment. The plants provide shade and absorb the heat of the sun, making tropical climates cooler. The roots of plants hold the soil together and absorb water, which helps to prevent flooding during heavy rainstorms.

Rainforest resources

One of the most valuable features of the rain forests is their huge selection of plant life, providing useful products such as food, timber and rubber. Many of the plants are also valuable for their medicinal properties, and indigenous rainforest peoples have been using plants as cures for hundreds of years. Recently, scientists have begun exploring rain forests in search of new plants containing chemicals that might help to solve medical problems such as AIDS or cancer. Drugs derived from rainforest plants are already in use. For example, the bark of one type of tree in Cameroon is collected in large quantities to produce an anti-cancer drug.

As well as plants and animal life, rain forests provide many natural mineral resources. Some of the world's largest sources of iron, gold, aluminium, copper and oil are found under areas of rain forest. The economy of Nigeria has been helped enormously by the discovery of huge stores of oil under its rain forest, while in the Camisea region of the Peruvian Amazon, a new gas field has recently been discovered which holds an estimated 280 billion cubic metres of gas. Mining is big business and provides thousands of jobs, but it can also cause terrible damage and pollution in the rain forests.

▼ An iron-ore furnace in the Grande Carajas area of the Amazon rain forest, in Brazil.

Crash Landing

In 1967, a helicopter flying over the Amazon rain forest in Brazil was forced to crash land on a hill. On board was a geologist. While he waited to be rescued, he investigated the rocks on the hill. He found that they were made of high-grade iron ore. This area, called the Grande Carajas, is the world's largest deposit of iron ore and is now a large mining area. It is estimated that 18 billion tonnes of iron ore exist there.

History of Rainforest People

First people

It is thought that people first moved into rain forests about one million years ago. Some scientists think that these people came from savannah (grassland) areas surrounding the forests. Over tens of thousands of years, rainforest people became smaller in size as they adapted to their environment. Races of people who are small in stature are thought to be among the most ancient rainforest peoples and include the Pygmies of Africa, the so-called 'negritos' of Asia, the Onge people of the Andaman Islands and the Aeta of the northern Philippines.

Indigenous Peoples

There are hundreds of indigenous groups living in rain forests. In Brazil alone there are thought to be 140, each with a different language and culture. Changes in the rain forests have led to the disappearance of many groups. It is thought that about 1,000 South American Indian groups have disappeared during the twentieth century.

There is evidence that people have lived in Amazonia for the last 15,000–20,000 years, but these forests have probably been inhabited for just as long as others around the world.

▼ This pyramid was built by the Mayan culture, which flourished in the rain forests of southern Mexico and Central America between AD 300 and AD 800.

A Tuli landowner in Papua ▶ New Guinea, in his garden of medicinal plants. Rainforest people have known about medicinal plants for thousands of years.

Colonists

At the end of the fifteenth century, Europeans began to explore the world, searching for 'new lands' and for goods and resources to trade. By this time, the people of many different nations had already been travelling and trading with rainforest peoples for a very long time. For example, Indian and Chinese traders had been sailing between the rainforest islands of Southeast Asia for over a thousand years. Rainforest people themselves were also on the move. In Amazonia and Africa, rainforest communities traded with people from other areas.

Rainforest City

The city of Belem in Brazil is on the Amazon river. In the eighteenth century, Belem was a small fishing settlement. Today, it is a huge city with a population of over one million. Belem's dramatic development began with the 'rubber boom', which occurred between about 1890 and 1910. During these years, rubber from wild Amazonian trees was in great demand for the manufacture of tyres for motor vehicles.

▼ The city of Belem is a wealthy port on the Amazon river, because goods such as timber and Brazil nuts are exported from there.

The arrival of Europeans had a dramatic effect. In just a few decades, the populations of indigenous peoples were reduced sharply by new diseases brought from Europe, and by slave-labour and cruel treatment. This happened in the Moluccas, or 'Spice Islands', of Indonesia. The Moluccas were the source of spices such as cloves and nutmeg, which were highly profitable to the spice trade. The islands were colonized by the Portuguese at the end of the fifteenth century, and the colonists treated the indigenous people appallingly. The Banda Islands had a population of around 15,000 when the Portuguese arrived. Within a few years, this had fallen to just 1,000 because many islanders had been executed, sold as slaves, or had committed suicide.

Over the last 500 years, people from Europe and elsewhere have colonized many countries which contain rain forests, and have brought different lifestyles to the forests. They have exploited resources such as timber, rubber, minerals, spices and oil, set up plantations and mines, built settlements, roads and railways, and introduced Christianity. More recently, migrants from within rainforest countries, as well as from abroad, have moved to rainforest areas.

▲ Gold mining in Brazil. The valuable mineral resources that first attracted European settlers to rainforest areas are still important to rainforest economies today.

The twentieth century

It is during the twentieth century that the greatest changes to rain forests have taken place. Many new towns and cities have been built, providing modern facilities from shopping malls to hospitals and leisure complexes. Millions of people are still trying to escape poverty and overcrowding by migrating to rainforest areas in search of land on which to grow food. In some countries, like Brazil, government programmes encourage people to move to the rain forests. Jobs in ranching, agriculture, mining and logging attract workers from other areas to live in the rain forest.

Transmigration

Since the 1950s, the Indonesian Government has been carrying out an enormous project, moving millions of people from the over-populated islands of Java and Bali to the Outer Islands. So far, nearly 7 million people, known as transmigrants, have been settled in Sumatra, Kalimantan, Sulawesi, Nusa Tenggara and Irian Jaya.

▼ This family have recently arrived on the rainforest island of Kalimantan, Indonesia. They were moved from their home on the crowded island of Java, as part of the Indonesian Government's Transmigration programme.

The transmigration scheme is intended to ease the population pressure on Java and Bali and to encourage development in rainforest areas. But there are many problems. The transmigrants burn huge areas of forest for farming, and many indigenous people have been pushed off their land. In 1997, a massive disaster happened on Kalimantan when huge forest fires burned over several months, blocking out the sun and filling the air with thick smoke. The rains failed to arrive and vast areas of rain forest were destroyed.

Snakes in the Night

A rubber tapper working in the Brazilian rain forest in 1908, wrote in his diary: 'My main trouble now was boa constrictors [snakes]… visiting me pretty near every night… They come crawling along noiselessly and roll their body up alongside the hammock laying their heads on one's chest, from time to time sticking their tongue in the corner of one's eye or mouth, then sticking their head, which is ice-cold, under one's arm pit.'

▼ Pictured in the 1890s, this group of Amazon rainforest Indians is typical of many who were captured by European colonists during the rubber boom and forced to work as slaves.

17

Work in Rain Forests

For most traditional rainforest peoples, work is not just one activity, but a number of activities related to getting food, raising their families and looking after their homes.

Hunting and fishing

For many rainforest dwellers, hunting and fishing are the main ways of obtaining their own food, and perhaps some extra to sell. For example, in the markets of Lagos, the capital of Nigeria, 'bush meat' from the rain forest is on sale every day.

▼ Two boys fishing in Indonesia, using scoop nets and a traditional trap made from rattan and bamboo fibres.

Rainforest animals are also hunted for their skins, like the jaguar in Colombia and the crocodile in Africa. In parts of India, endangered sloth bears are hunted illegally so that parts of their bodies can be used for Chinese medicine.

In mangrove areas, like the mouth of the Ganges river in Bangladesh and in coastal Ecuador, many people make a living from catching fish and shellfish and farming shrimps. Fishing for salmon is traditional and is still important for peoples of the north-west coast of North America, like the Tlingit and the Haisla.

Rainforest gardens

Millions of rainforest people – whether indigenous or not – spend much of their time collecting wild foods and firewood and tending small gardens cut out of the forest. These rainforest gardens occur throughout the world. Usually, a small area of forest is cut down and the branches and wood are burnt. The wood ash that is left helps the crops to grow. The area is then planted with many different crops, such as cassava (a root vegetable) in South America, yams (a vegetable similar to the potato) in tropical Africa and maize in Central America. Bananas and other fruit trees like mangoes are also planted.

▲ Children harvesting chilli peppers in a typical rainforest garden in Nigeria.

Collecting rainforest products

Millions of people are employed in collecting, transporting and processing products from rain forests. These products include raffia in Madagascar, jalapeño chilli peppers in Central America and swallowtail butterflies from Indonesia, which are sold to tourists. In Southeast Asia, the rope-like stems of rattan palms are collected all year round by local people. About half a million people make their living by harvesting and processing the rattan stems, which are mostly used to make furniture.

Longest Rattan Stem
The longest rattan stem found so far measured 244 metres.

◀ This man has been gathering rattan cane from the rain forests of Kalimantan, in Indonesia.

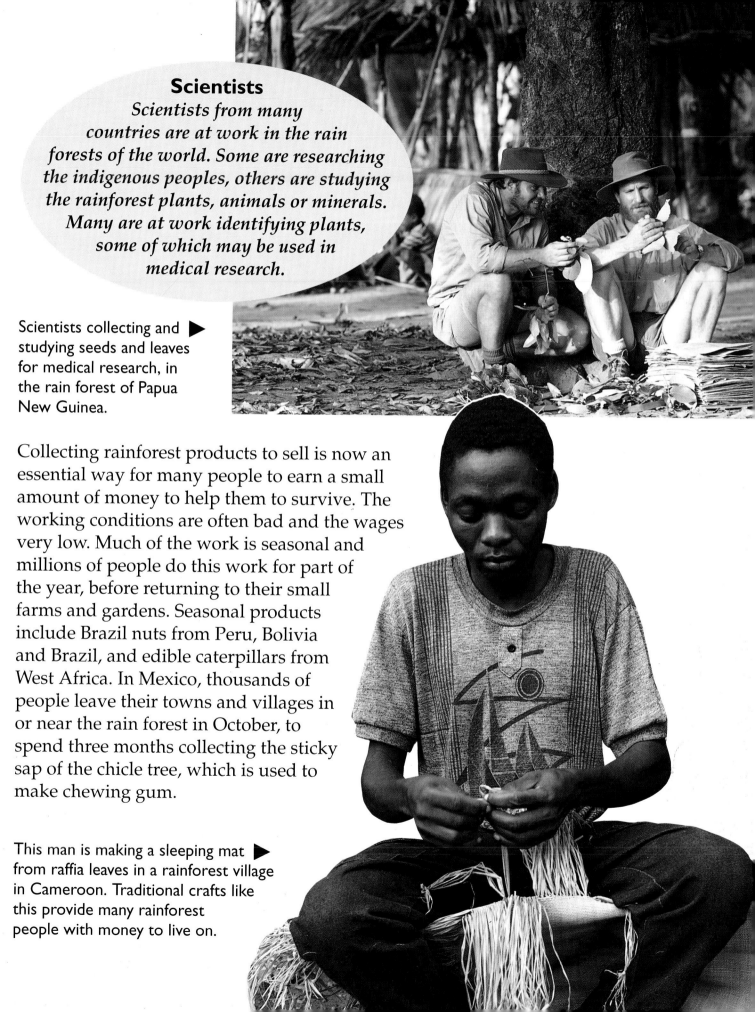

Scientists

Scientists from many countries are at work in the rain forests of the world. Some are researching the indigenous peoples, others are studying the rainforest plants, animals or minerals. Many are at work identifying plants, some of which may be used in medical research.

Scientists collecting and ▶ studying seeds and leaves for medical research, in the rain forest of Papua New Guinea.

Collecting rainforest products to sell is now an essential way for many people to earn a small amount of money to help them to survive. The working conditions are often bad and the wages very low. Much of the work is seasonal and millions of people do this work for part of the year, before returning to their small farms and gardens. Seasonal products include Brazil nuts from Peru, Bolivia and Brazil, and edible caterpillars from West Africa. In Mexico, thousands of people leave their towns and villages in or near the rain forest in October, to spend three months collecting the sticky sap of the chicle tree, which is used to make chewing gum.

This man is making a sleeping mat ▶ from raffia leaves in a rainforest village in Cameroon. Traditional crafts like this provide many rainforest people with money to live on.

▲ A worker at an oil palm plantation in Malaysia loading palm fruit into containers, ready to be taken to the factory.

Working on plantations

In tropical rain forests, big businesses and landowners have set up large plantations, producing products like African oil palm, rubber, coffee, pineapples, nutmegs and cloves. Although plantations provide employment for both local people and migrants, the conditions and pay are usually very poor. For example, on rainforest tea plantations in China, rubber plantations in Malaysia and oil palm plantations in West Africa, people must work long hours with just a few days off each year. Processing factories set up near plantations also provide employment, but working conditions inside are often hot and very uncomfortable.

A good example of a profitable plantation crop is African palm oil. Throughout West Africa, Southeast Asia and South America, large plantations of African oil palm have been established in rainforest areas. The fruits and their seeds produce two kinds of oil which are used in large quantities for a variety of products, from biscuits to perfume and soap. African oil palms are now the world's most important source of oils.

◀ A worker on a pineapple plantation on the Ivory Coast.

23

▲ A cowboy in Brazil looking after a herd of cattle on land that was once rain forest.

Ranching and logging

Two industries that have had a big effect on rainforest areas are ranching and logging. Since the 1970s, much rain forest in South and Central America has been cut down and burnt to make way for cattle ranches. Most of these produce beef to supply wealthy countries such as the USA. Ranching earns a lot of money in rainforest areas, but it provides jobs for very few people, since most cattle herds can be looked after by a small number of herders on horseback.

The activity of logging companies is having the greatest single effect on forests worldwide. Heavy machines do much of the felling and processing, but large numbers of people are employed. In Canada and Australia, foresters generally operate heavy machinery such as harvesters, cranes and giant saws, but in places like Gabon and the Solomon Islands, people do many of the jobs by hand.

▼ Alaskan timber is floated down the river to this mill, where it is cut into planks or pulped to make paper.

Alaska

More than one-third of the northern US state of Alaska is forested, and running along the coast is an area of temperate rain forest containing some of the largest trees on earth. These forests are currently being cut down so that the logs can be sold to Asian countries, mainly Japan, to be used to make paper and plastics. Thousands of people work in the timber industry and Alaska exports around 450,000 m³ of wood a year.

Transport and Communications

Rain forests today still include some of the last truly wild places on earth. They have remained wild largely because they are difficult to travel in. The combination of dense vegetation, heavy rains, steep slopes and swampy soils continues to create a barrier to rapid travel. In many rainforest areas of the world, travelling on foot is often the only way to get around.

◀ These Wayana Indian children from French Guiana travel to school by motorized canoe each day.

Rivers as roads

Rivers have been, and still are, the most important highways in rain forests. For millions of rainforest people, canoes with motors or oars are an extremely important means of travel. Logging, mining and other companies often use huge boats to transport products out of the rain forest to ports and factories.

A boat arriving in Belem, Brazil, with a cargo of Brazil nuts for processing may have travelled 5,000 km upstream when it arrives.

On large rivers, and for trips between rainforest islands, passenger ferries are widely used. A huge variety of other water-craft are also used in rainforest areas including hovercraft, motor boats and even jet skis. There is a growing number of tourist boats on rainforest rivers, especially in tourist areas like parts of Thailand.

Traditional Boats
Many indigenous rainforest people still use hollowed-out tree-trunks to make boats. The Maori of New Zealand and the Tlingit of Alaska make wooden boats that can be used on the ocean. In the Amazon and African rain forests, canoes are still made from tree-trunks.

▲ Drying out a freshly carved canoe, made from the trunk of a rainforest tree.

▼ A passenger ferry on the Amazon river in Brazil.

▲ Constructing a road through the Brazilian Amazon. The road will link the Brazilian cities of Manaus and Boa Vista with Venezuela.

Roads through the rain forest

Road travel is relatively new to rain forests. It is not easy to build and maintain roads in such hot, wet conditions. Heavy rains often wash roads away and some are only passable for a few months of the year. In some rainforest areas, the roads have to be re-laid after each rainy season. Most rainforest roads are still not paved.

Most people generally travel along roads on overcrowded buses or lorries. The operators of industries such as logging and mining often have to build their own roads to transport raw materials. It is usually only very wealthy people who travel by private car. A more affordable means of transport is the bicycle.

A walkway in the treetops of the rain ▶ forest in Borneo, Malaysia.

Maintaining roads in rainforest areas is very difficult because the forest vegetation grows so quickly. Roads can become overgrown in only a few months if not looked after. Even insects like ants can make roads impassable. Some types of ant look for flat areas of soft earth in which to make their underground nests, which can be 100 m across. They often choose rainforest roads, which sometimes cave in because of the enormous network of chambers and tunnels under the road. This has even happened to the huge Trans-Amazonian highway in Brazil.

The children of workers on an oil palm ▶ plantation in Cameroon, walking to school. Roads are often built by large companies, to provide transport for crops, timber and industrial products.

Railways

There are railways in various rainforest areas of the world, but they are much less common than roads and generally much less important than rivers for passenger transport. Many railways were built to transport raw materials. One of the newest and most ambitious railways cuts through the rain forest of Gabon in Africa, linking the capital city, Libreville with the important mining town of Franceville.

▲ Local people and tourists waiting for a train that runs from San Antonio to Porto Velho in the Amazon.

Air travel

Travel by aeroplane and helicopter has opened up areas of rain forest that could once only be reached by weeks of walking or boat travel. For example, travel between the rainforest islands of the Solomons is only possible by aeroplane or boat. Dotted across the world's rain forests there are now thousands of small, unpaved runways where light aircraft can land. Geologists from oil and mining companies often travel to remote areas by helicopter or small aircraft to carry out surveys. Tourists, missionaries and government officials all make use of this form of travel. For most rainforest people, however, air travel is too expensive.

▼ A helicopter delivering an electricity generator to a rainforest village in Brazil.

In the coastal rainforest areas of New Zealand and Tasmania, the only quick way to travel is by helicopter. In the forests of New Zealand, some large trees that have been cut for their timber are air-lifted out because there are no logging roads.

▼ Asian elephants at work in the timber industry of Lampang Province, Thailand. The Asian elephant is an endangered species.

Homes and Settlements

▲ The roof of this house is thatched with palm leaves.

▼ A woman preparing bush meat outside her mud house in a rainforest village in Cameroon.

Traditional homes

Indigenous rainforest people live in many different sorts of traditional buildings. The number of people who live in each house and the sort of settlements they make up also varies.

Some of the smallest and simplest dwellings are the huts used for part of the year by the Baka Pygmies of Cameroon. These individual family huts are made from a framework of small branches, covered with overlapping leaves. The Penan of Sarawak are another nomadic people who use simple shelters that can be abandoned and rebuilt as required. The Mehinaku Indians of Brazil, on the other hand, build huge, dome-shaped houses up to 40 m long, with grass roofs. The men of many different families work together to build each house, which will have room for about thirty people to live comfortably inside.

The materials used to build traditional shelters vary from forest to forest, depending on what is locally available. For example, in the Nigerian rain forest some people live in houses with clay walls while, in the cool rain forests on the Pacific coast of North America, planks cut from giant trees such as cedars are used to make some traditional houses.

▼ A Dyak longhouse in Borneo.

Longhouses

Longhouses are the traditional homes of the Dyak peoples of Borneo, and can house up to 100 families. Each family has its own front door and a private area inside, with storerooms, a sleeping area and a kitchen at the back. The front of the longhouse has a wide, open, porch-like area running its length where social activities take place. Longhouses are often built almost entirely of plentiful local bamboo.

▲ Village children playing in front of their stilt huts in a village in the Philippines.

Making a Mbuti Hut

The Mbuti Pygmies live in the rain forest of Central Africa. The women make their huts by fixing a ring of young trees in the ground and twining the tops together. Branches are then woven into the framework and layers of leaves are attached to make the hut waterproof. Finally, the huts are secured with larger branches so they do not blow away in strong winds.

Many rainforest houses are built on stilts. Wooden stilt-houses are often found in coastal areas, or where there is likely to be flooding. In the Philippines, the stilt houses of the Badajao people stand in sheltered coastal waters and are connected by slender poles. On dry land, raising a house above the ground provides rainforest dwellers with protection against wild creatures and separates them from domestic animals such as pigs and chickens.

New houses

Today, people who are not traditional rainforest dwellers often build houses that are unsuitable for the local conditions. These often have cement walls and corrugated iron roofs, which heat up the inside of the house during the day. When heavy rain falls on the metal roof, the sound inside the house is deafening. Many indigenous forest people are now living in these houses too, because they have been forced to change their way of life. This kind of house is the most common for people in rainforest towns and cities. In places like Manila in the Philippines, or Cairns in Australia, wealthy people live in houses or blocks of flats that are well built, with air-conditioning to keep them cool.

A few buildings, such as those built specially for ecotourists, use the latest technology to provide comfortable living quarters without damaging the environment. This involves using solar power, collecting rainwater for drinking and using special toilets to protect the environment.

▼ Modern flats in a clearing in the Amazon rain forest, near the city of Belem.

Inside rainforest houses

Indigenous rainforest people generally use materials that they gather themselves to build and furnish their homes. These may include strong, rot-resistant timbers, strips of bark and thatch made from palm leaves. Fibres stripped from palm and other leaves, as well as vines and canes are used to make things like mats, baskets and sieves. Hammocks made from cotton or other plant fibres are popular throughout Central and South America. They are much cooler than beds and are just as popular in towns and cities as they are in remote forest areas.

▼ A young girl swings in a hammock in a mangrove village in southern Mexico.

▼ Settlers in a rainforest area of Guatemala, building a home in a clearing where they plan to set up a farm.

Leisure and Tourism

Many rainforest people have to work very hard for most of the week, but when they have some free time they might spend it in a variety of ways. For the wealthy, the number of leisure activities is endless; there is water skiing, yachting, the cinema, rock concerts, shopping and restaurants. Poorer people do not usually have much free time. A day off is likely to be spent sleeping or just being with the family. Most people working in the rain forest enjoy celebrating religious holidays, watching television and playing football.

Mayan Basketball
Over 1,000 years ago, the Mayas in Mexico played a game called ollamaltitzli, *which was similar to the modern game of basketball. The players kept the ball off the ground using their feet and elbows. The idea of the game was to get the ball through a stone hoop set high on a wall.*

▼ A group of men playing a game of checkers in the rainforest city of Belem, Brazil.

Traditional pastimes

Leisure time, as we know it, would be a puzzle to many traditional rainforest people. Time not spent gardening or preparing food, for example, is often used for making useful tools, playing with the children or telling stories. Traditional activities include swimming, making pots and wrestling. Football is also becoming very popular.

▼ For many rainforest children, there are few toys. These boys in the Philippines have a home-made bicycle.

▲ A game of football on the Cook Islands of Polynesia.

Television and radio

In all but the remotest parts of rain forests, it is possible to watch television and listen to the radio. Some rainforest towns in Alaska, Mexico and Australia have their own local television and radio stations, but most now have either cable or satellite television. In wealthy villages, every house may have a television set. In the poorest parts of many rain forests, a town's restaurants are often the only places where people can watch television.

Sport

Travelling through a rain forest in Central America or West Africa, it is possible to see football pitches close to many villages. Football is very popular and is often part of school activities. Many other types of sport are also popular. For example, villages in the mangrove forests of Mexico usually have football and volleyball pitches, while in Bangladesh the most common women's sport is badminton. Because of their climate and landscape, swimming is popular throughout the world's rain forests. It is a practical skill as well as a pastime, and rainforest children usually learn to swim at an early age.

Festivals and music

Many religious festivals are celebrated in rainforest villages and towns, and celebrations and festivals are held to mark important events. On particular days, the whole community joins together to mark an important event or to give thanks for a good harvest. These celebrations are very happy occasions, with music and dancing, and can last for many days. Women often work together to supply food and drink for a whole village, as well as visiting guests.

Ju Ju Men

The Ju Ju man can be seen at many traditional West African ceremonies. He is usually dressed in a one-piece body suit so that the other villagers do not know who he is. In Cameroon and Nigerian rainforest communities, the Ju Ju man of the Ekpe religion performs dances as the leopard spirit.

▼ Four men of the Yagua people of Colombia playing traditional drums.

A Ju Ju man dressed as a leopard spirit in a remote ▶ rainforest village in Cameroon.

41

▲ For those who can afford them, there are now modern leisure activities in rain forests, such as jet-skiing.

Leisure for workers

Some of the best sports facilities in rain forests are those found at remote oil wells, power plants and mines. In the Brazilian rain forest, at the massive Tucurui Dam project, an entire town was built specially for the workers. It is fenced with barbed wire to keep local people away, but inside there are bars, cinemas, swimming pools and tennis courts.

At remote oil drilling platforms in places like Sarawak, leisure facilities such as tennis and squash courts and a social club have to be built before engineers will agree to work on a new drilling platform.

Tourism

Over the last twenty years, the number of tourists visiting rainforest areas has been growing. It is now popular to visit rain forests on holiday or as part of a luxury cruise. Hotels in rain forests even organize treks to see wildlife and traditional ways of life.

Tourism provides employment in rainforest regions, and in some areas it has become the main form of employment. However, it has led to a change in lifestyle for many rainforest people. The advantages of tourism are that it increases people's awareness of the lifestyle of indigenous rainforest people and of the fragile environment. However, some indigenous peoples resent the fact that some traditional villages now exist only as places for tourists to visit.

▼ Tourists on a guided trek in the rain forest of Ecuador. Ecotourism brings visitors to rainforest areas to learn about the forest and its plants, animals and indigenous peoples.

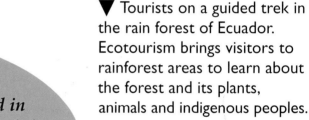

Work in Tourism
Millions of people are already employed in tourism in rainforest areas, and it is predicted that the number of jobs will continue to increase. Jobs range from work in hotels and restaurants, to acting as guides, showing visitors rare rainforest animals and plants.

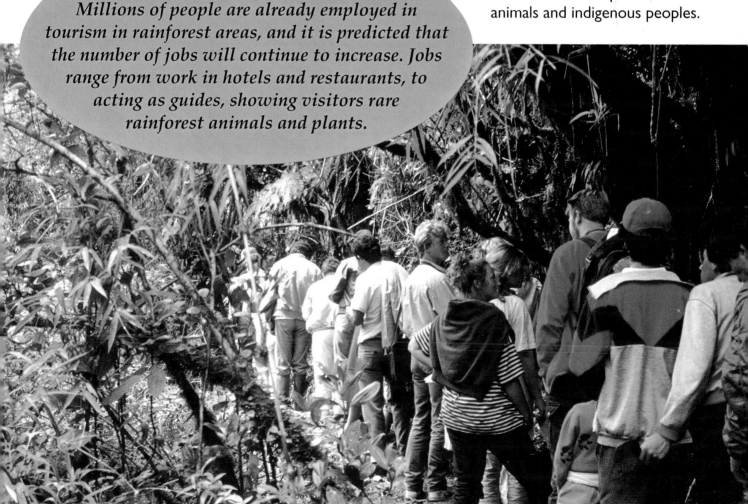

The Future

Rain forests are important to everyone in the world, whether they live in the rain forests or not. But they are disappearing at an alarming pace. The world's population is increasing at a rate of one million people every four days. This has two effects on rain forests: more rainforest products are needed to support the population, while increasing numbers of people are moving to rainforest areas. All this has increased the destruction of the forests. Urgent action is required to slow down the loss of rain forests if they are to survive for long into the twenty-first century.

Protecting the forests

There are many ways of protecting the rain forests. National Parks have been set up in countries like Australia, Cameroon and Thailand, to control the use of the forests and to protect the plants and animals. There is also growing pressure for the proper management of rain forests. This means taking products such as timber, spices and nuts without seriously damaging the forest.

▼ Penan people in Malaysia blocking a road used by a logging company. Many Penan people have been arrested and put in prison for trying to stop loggers destroying their homes.

These children in Cameroon ▶ are learning about the forest where they live so that they can protect it for the future.

International interest
People all around the world are becoming more aware of the need to preserve the rain forests. Campaigns have been organized to stop deforestation and to get large companies and governments to recognize the rights of rainforest people.

Fighting for the forests
Many rainforest people are trying desperately to save their homes and their livelihoods. The struggle has sometimes ended in violence. In 1989, Chico Mendes was killed because he organized protests against the destruction of the rain forest of the Brazilian Amazon.

The way forward
Environmental groups are campaigning to make sure that rain forests are protected. They also want the remaining forests to be managed so that they are not destroyed. Then the rain forests can go on to provide raw materials for future generations. Many of the groups help schoolchildren learn more about the rain forests by printing leaflets and booklets for schools. You could try contacting them using the addresses given on page 47.

Glossary

Atmosphere The gases that surround the earth (or other planets).

Bush meat A term used widely in Africa referring to meat from wild animals.

Colonized Occupied by people who have moved to a new area to live.

Deforestation The clearing of trees from a forest area.

Descendants People who are descended from previous generations.

Economy A country's financial system.

Ecotourists People who visit natural environments with an interest in conserving them.

Endangered At risk of dying out.

Environment Our surroundings, including the landscape, animals and plants.

Equator An imaginary line around the earth, midway between the North and South Poles.

Flooded forest A forest which is flooded permanently or at certain times of the year.

Furnace A building where very high temperatures are generated.

Geologist A person who studies rocks and the landscape.

Indigenous Belonging originally or naturally to a particular place.

Mangrove forest Evergreen forest found along some tropical coastlines and in swamps.

Migrants People who move from their homes to another area or country.

Mineral A substance such as oil, coal or metal that is obtained by mining.

Missionaries People who travel to places in order to spread a religious message.

Nomadic A way of describing people who do not have any one home location but move regularly.

Ore A rock from which useful substances can be obtained.

Plantations Areas in which single crops are planted, often in rows.

Pollution Damage to the environment.

Raw materials The materials from which manufactured goods are made.

Solar power Power generated from the heat of the Sun.

Species A group of plants or animals of the same type that share similar characteristics.

Temperate A mild or moderate climate.

Tropics The area between the Tropics of Cancer and Capricorn, which has high temperatures and rainfall.

Further Information

Books to read

Habitats: Forests by Anita Ganeri (Wayland, 1996)

The Last Rainforest edited by Mark Collins (Mitchell Beazley, 1995)

Mad about Tropical Rainforests (Friends of the Earth, 1996)

People and Places in Peril: Rainforests by Sara Oldfield (Cherrytree Books, 1995)

Rainforest Amerindians by Anna Lewington (Wayland, 1992)

Sacha Mama – Mother Jungle: Eco-Tourism in the Amazonian Rainforest (education pack) (ActionAid, 1997)

Wayland Atlas of Rain Forests by Anna Lewington (Wayland, 1996)

Wayland Atlas of Threatened Cultures (Wayland, 1996

What do we know about Amazonian Indians by Anna Lewington (MacDonald Young Books, 1993)

World of the Rainforest by Rosie McCormick (TwoCan, 1997)

CD Roms
Exploring Land Habitats (Wayland, 1997)

Useful addresses

Friends of The Earth (UK)
26–28 Underwood Street,
London N1 7JQ
Tel: 0171 490 1555
Internet: www.for.co.uk/

Living Earth Foundation
4 Great James St,
London WC1N 3DA
Tel: 0171 242 3816
Internet: http://www.gn.apc.org/LivingEarth

Reforest The Earth
42–46 Bethel Street,
Norwich NR2 1NR
Tel: 01603 611953

Survival International
11–15 Emerald Street,
London WC1N 3QL
Tel: 0171 242 1441
Internet: www.survival.org

World Wide Fund For Nature
Panda House,
Weyside Park,
Catteshall Lane
Godalming,
Surrey GU7 1XR
Tel:01608 676691
Internet: http://www.wwf–uk.org

Picture acknowledgements
The publisher would like to thank the following for allowing their pictures to be used in this book: Bruce Coleman 20; Environmental Images 44; Getty Images *Title page,* 5, 7, 9 (both), 21 (top), 25, 37; Impact 30 (bottom), 40; Panos 16, 23, 32 (top), 33, 34, 38, 41 (left), 42; Edward Parker 7 (top), 21 (bottom), 24, 29 (bottom), 32 (bottom), 36, 41 (right); Planet Earth 13; South American Pictures 14, 17, 26, 27 (top), 30 (top); Still Pictures *Cover,* Chapter openers, 4, 5 (top), 8, 10, 11, 15, 18, 19, 22, 28, 29 (top), 31, 39, 43, 45; Wayland Picture Library 12.

Index

Numbers in **bold** refer to photographs.